DUMP TRUCKS

by Katie Chanez

Cody Koala
An Imprint of Pop!
popbooksonline.com

abdobooks.com

Published by Pop!, a division of ABDO, PO Box 398166, Minneapolis, Minnesota 55419. Copyright © 2020 by POP, LLC. International copyrights reserved in all countries. No part of this book may be reproduced in any form without written permission from the publisher. Pop!™ is a trademark and logo of POP, LLC.

Printed in the United States of America, North Mankato, Minnesota

052019
092019
THIS BOOK CONTAINS RECYCLED MATERIALS

Cover Photo: Shutterstock Images
Interior Photos: Shutterstock Images, 1, 18–19, 20; iStockphoto, 5, 7 (top), 7 (bottom left), 7 (bottom right), 8, 11, 13, 15, 17, 21

Editor: Meg Gaertner
Series Designer: Sophie Geister-Jones

Library of Congress Control Number: 2018964594

Publisher's Cataloging-in-Publication Data
Names: Chanez, Katie, author.
Title: Dump trucks / by Katie Chanez.
Description: Minneapolis, Minnesota : Pop!, 2020 | Series: Construction vehicles | Includes online resources and index.
Identifiers: ISBN 9781532163319 (lib. bdg.) | ISBN 9781644940044 (pbk.) | ISBN 9781532164750 (ebook)
Subjects: LCSH: Dump trucks--Juvenile literature. | Construction equipment --Juvenile literature. | Construction industry--Equipment and supplies --Juvenile literature.
Classification: DDC 629.225--dc23

Hello! My name is

Cody Koala

Pop open this book and you'll find QR codes like this one, loaded with information, so you can learn even more!

Scan this code* and others like it while you read, or visit the website below to make this book pop.

popbooksonline.com/dump-trucks

*Scanning QR codes requires a web-enabled smart device with a QR code reader app and a camera.

Table of Contents

Chapter 1
The Dump Truck Can Help!. . 4

Chapter 2
A Dump Truck's Job 6

Chapter 3
Parts of a Dump Truck . . . 10

Chapter 4
Types of Dump Trucks . . . 16

Making Connections 22
Glossary. 23
Index 24
Online Resources 24

Chapter 1

The Dump Truck Can Help!

Construction workers need to fill a hole. They need dirt. A dump truck brings them the dirt. It pours the dirt into the hole.

Watch a video here!

5

Chapter 2

A Dump Truck's Job

Different building jobs need different **materials**. Dump trucks carry materials such as sand, dirt, or rocks. They bring these materials to construction areas.

Complete an activity here!

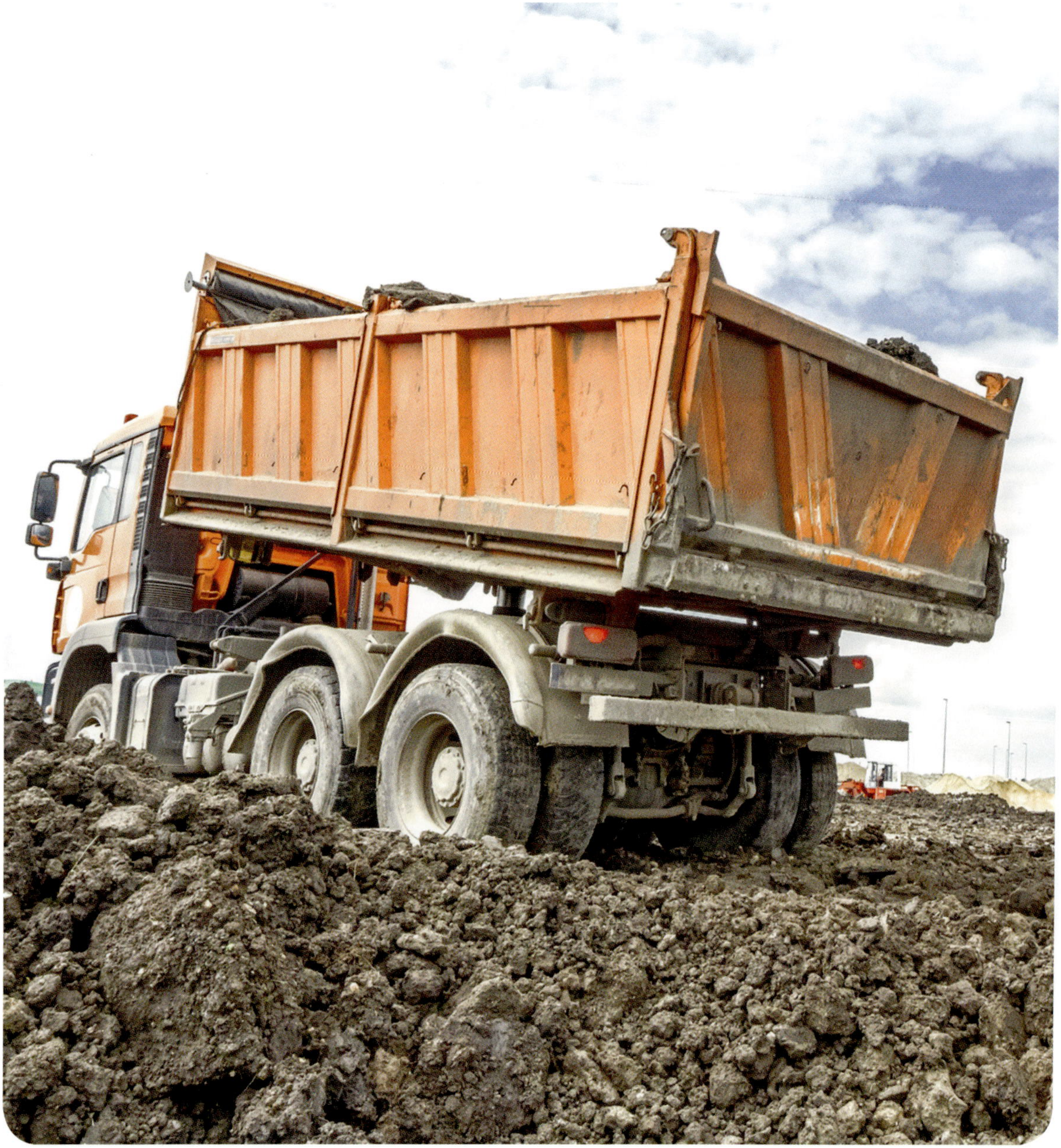

Sometimes construction workers have too much dirt or **debris**. They need to get rid of it. Dump trucks take the debris away.

Chapter 3

Parts of a Dump Truck

Dump trucks have many parts. The truck moves on wheels. It is very strong. It can carry heavy **loads** without breaking.

Learn more here!

The **dump bed** holds the **materials**. Most dump beds have a back door that can swing. The door locks into place to keep materials in the bed. The door opens when it is time to dump.

> Before there were dump trucks, carts pulled by horses did the same work.

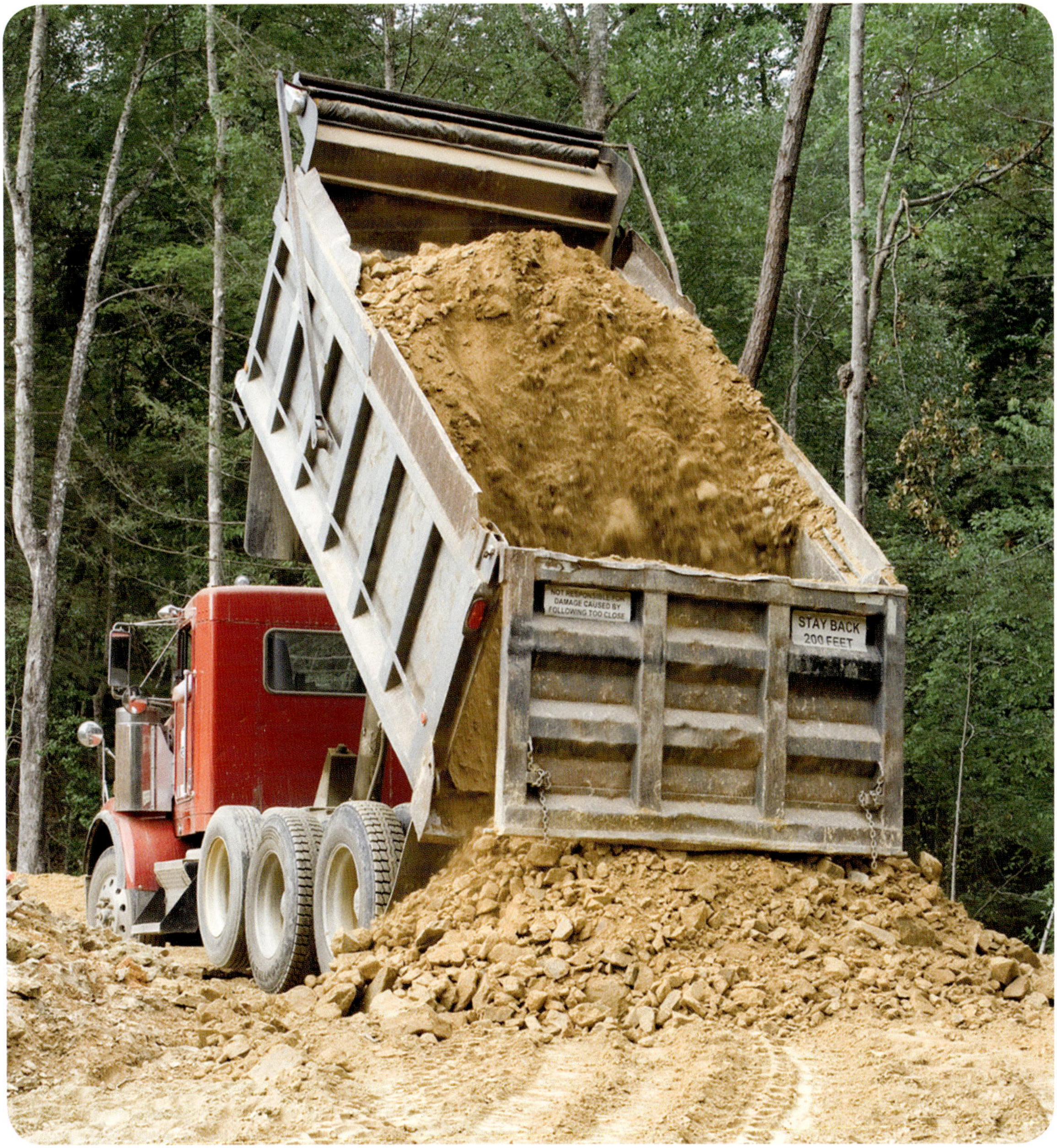
DAMAGE CAUSED BY
FOLLOWING TOO CLOSE
STAY BACK
200 FEET

Under the dump bed is a pump. The pump lifts. It pushes one end of the dump bed up. This makes the materials fall out of the other end.

> The truck driver can control the pump from inside the truck.

dump bed

truck

pump

swinging door

Chapter 4

Types of Dump Trucks

There are different types of dump trucks. **Mining** dump trucks carry the biggest **loads**. They can carry the weight of more than 70 elephants!

Learn more here!

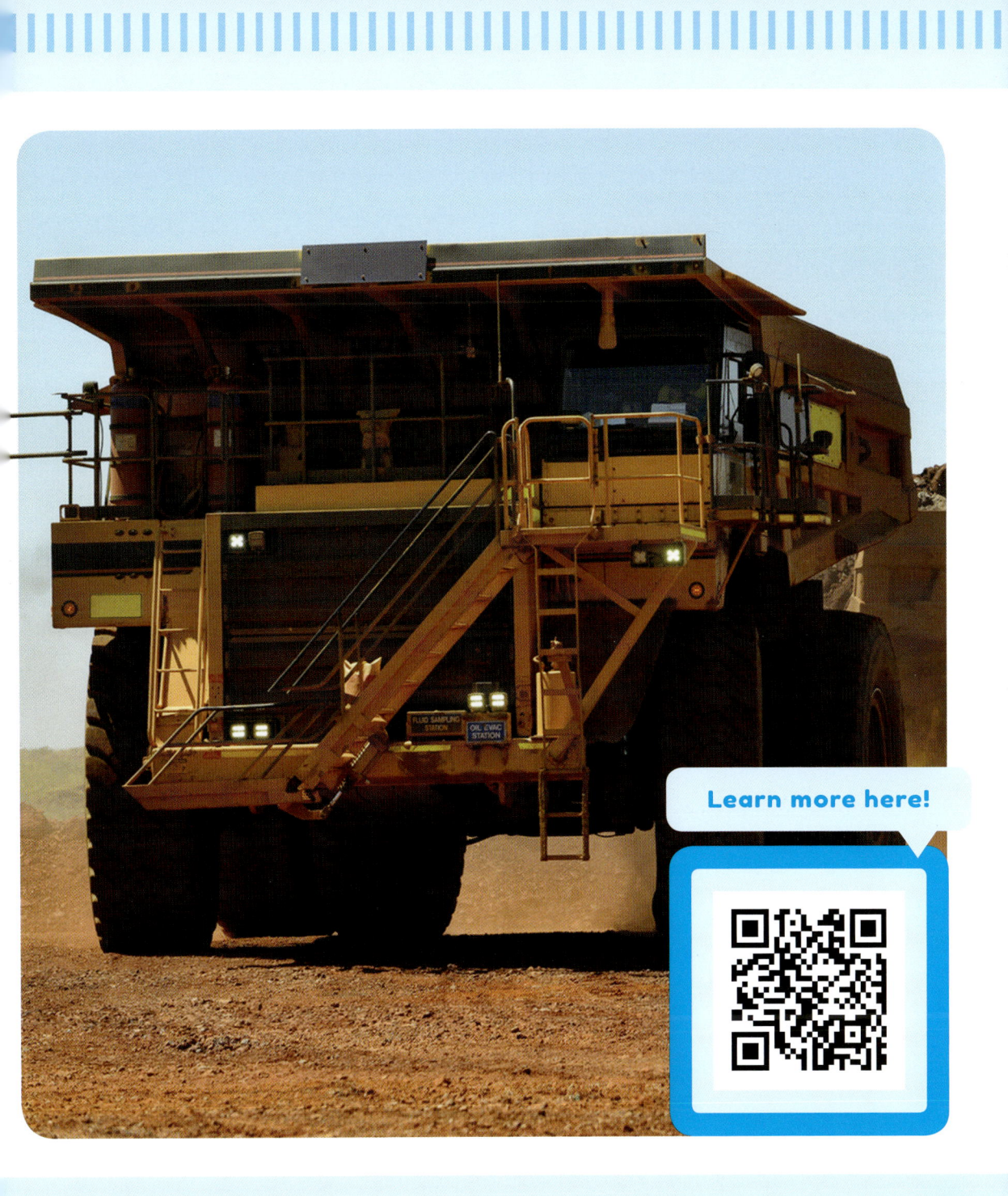

17

Most dump trucks dump out of the back of the truck. They use a swinging door.

But some trucks can dump to the side of the truck.

Some dump trucks open at the bottom of the **dump bed**. **Materials** fall through.

These dump trucks help build roads. They deliver the right materials for the roads.

Making Connections

Text-to-Self

Have you ever seen a dump truck at work? What was it carrying?

Text-to-Text

Have you read about other construction vehicles? How are they similar to dump trucks? How are they different?

Text-to-World

Dump trucks move things from one place to another. What other vehicles can be used to move things?

Glossary

debris – waste items that are no longer useful.

dump bed – the part of a dump truck that holds the materials.

load – the object that is being carried.

material – something that another thing can be made from.

mining – related to the process of digging rocks or minerals from the ground.

Index

debris, 9

doors, 12, 15, 18

dump beds, 12, 14, 15, 20

loads, 10, 16

materials, 6, 12, 14, 20–21

mining, 16

pumps, 14, 15

wheels, 10

Online Resources
popbooksonline.com

Thanks for reading this Cody Koala book!

Scan this code* and others like it in this book, or visit the website below to make this book pop!

popbooksonline.com/dump-trucks

*Scanning QR codes requires a web-enabled smart device with a QR code reader app and a camera.